POETRY NOW

WALES

1992

First published in Great Britain in 1992 by
POETRY NOW
4 Hythegate, Werrington,
Peterborough, PE4 7ZP

Contents

Dole Drums

When I consider how my giro's spent
before the week's half up and how I've tried
to make it last all fortnight and grown tired
of hassling the council for my rent,

it makes me think it's high time I turned bent
and sold my arse or robbed a bank or lied
about the few quid I've made on the side
from baling hay. But Thatcher, to prevent

that murmur, soon replies; 'The state's no need
of either your work or your gifts; you'd best
accept retirement at the standard rate

on offer with good grace. For where there's greed
and discontent, it might affect the rest
whose only option is to stand and wait'.

Geoffrey Constable

1

Through the Glass Darkly

Earth's womb, dark cradle,
swells the life within;
translated form of immanent ideas
by sense perceived.
Before it is, it was.

energy of light untold,
hardened to our past,
shouts through the melting atom.
The eloquent rock
tells us the forward way.

Time is the great illusion
of our mortality.
The power that through the shoot
becomes the flower
is the reality.

Harry Stevenson

Old Unc

I saw in my face
A change taking place
On my wrinkly brow
I'm a lot older now

With watery eyes
Reflect all my sighs
Seventy years have gone by
Single memories survive

Time takes it's toll
The triumphs and goals
Grant peace in my mind
Make it all worthwhile

I know I shall die
My heart will not cry
The child I leave
Continues to be me

M Sims

The Workmen

They said they'd come at half past ten
And now it's ten past one
Waiting in for workmen isn't
My idea of fun!
Then unapologetically
They land outside my door
With just time for five cups of tea
Before down tools at four!
Why are workmen always late?
They're such a tardy bunch
Why do they say they'll come at eight
Then turn up after lunch?
Do they have trouble getting up?
Or can't they tell the time?
Perhaps they're playing games with me
I think that it's a crime!
But wait, it's only half past one
At last, here come the men
I'd better not say anything
In case they go again!

Clair Worsfold

The Long Women
(for Julie)

Elongated shadows on the mottled sand.
Legs like stalking clowns stilts.
Waves lapping over their dark heads.
Shimmering, like silky scarfs
Stretched taut in the naked light.

We walked along in silence,
In the early evening
When the beach was deserted
Save for an exhausted jogger or two.

The street lamps and car head lights
Glimmered upon the waves.
The sand, broken by the tyre marks
and foot prints.
Footprints of joggers and dog walkers
As well as ours.

As we walked by the sea in silence.

Lousie E Harrington

On the M56

Looking,
To the cold grey sky,
Which chokes silently,
Losing to the unrelenting chimney.
The moon,
Once a blinding light,
Is now a fading inconstant glow.
It's pulse vanishes and reappears,
A moment lost beyond the aching cloud.
Below,
The hazy lamplight,
Is a sore reminder,
An artificial illumination,
Which dismisses the darkness and natural sorrow.

John Wright

Eternity

When one of us
is strong enough to
say goodbye,
it will be without
tears and anger.
For
I shall never leave you
Nor
You leave me,.
we shall just lengthen the
time before we meet again,
passing through from this life
to meet in the next
as we did in the last.

Kim Hunter

Imagine

In my mind we still exist
As one of our hearts entwine
And in my mind I truly love
The one who can't be mine

All the years we have loved
Yet are not able to express
The fire burning deep within
Or the feelings of the tenderness

We meet from time to time
Drift into a different land
Our separate lives forgotten
Daring to hold each others hand

We will never hold our children
Or live our lives as one
But in our minds we do exist
Our affair goes on and on

Hannah Mortlock

Michelangelo

The sleek pulse of the cursor
has ceased to beat. There is a dark face
at the window of the world,
silence at the core.
Michelangelo, beautiful, deadly, sweeps
in like an angel, scrolls up
the page of thought, obliterating action.
There is no warning.
No line-noise on the wires
or sudden crash. Only, perhaps,
a rush of wind or wings
as he leaps across the programme,
infiltrates the pattern.
I have seen him work,
as if I stood below an artist
and watched his fingers move
quickly, defiantly, against
the logic of hands. He is savage,
decadent, burns to the centre
of the brain. Language unravels
with this strange dropped stitch of magic.
And suddenly I'm in an older time,
where chaos theory is one dropped leaf,
a butterfly's terrible movement,
and there is nothing
but splashed sun striking like a God.
I have a terror of this power,
infecting text, as body by disease.
Words toppling from the screen
will leave me speechless.

Kathy Miles

My Apple Tree

As I watched the last leaf fall, from the apple tree,
to wither, with the windfalls on the ground,
the tree may have sighed, before drawing the blind
and going into a long winter's sleep.

Some sadness comes over me,
recalling the spring of this year,
blossoms like ballerinas swaying in the breeze
or dancing madly in the wind,
heralding the crop to come.

The time is right, what a bountiful sight,
rosy apples chaperoned by green leaves,
waiting to be chosen before the fall,
often hastened by small boys climbing the wall,
hoping not to be seen at all.

The show is over, you want to be alone,
to grow within, ready for another spring.
Tho you are bare and unadorned, standing with dignity,
as a widow with memories of love,
I can learn much from you little tree.

That my living be worth while,
caring and sharing be my theme,
throw our a life line to some in need,
be remembered at mine end, for some good.

Try as I might it won't always be right, I'm human to the core,
but will be stronger for the fight,
if never reaching saintly heights,
if I follow in God's guiding light.

Katie Fox Williams

10

Reflections

The man looked into the eyes of the boy,
A beggar of seventeen summers.
There was nothing else for the lad to do
In the year of eighteen ninety two.

The woman looked into the eyes of the girl,
A beggar of seventeen summers.
There was little else the lass could do
In the year of nineteen ninety two.

Betty Lucking

I Lose you Again

I can see you above the soothing tree tops,
I can see you on the ancient lane,
On the desolate white chalky lane,
Throwing up dust and white memories;
I see for miles from my perch in the trees,
You will never be the same again.

The further you walk shimmering to my horizon,
The further my love for you will fade and die.
So alone, desperate and sure I will fade and die,
For the want of mere hours in your distant company,
I will sacrifice my sight so you can comfort me,
My strange vision falters and close I hear you sigh.

How dead we are to one another's feelings,
How dead cold, soft side by side but fathoms apart,
Floating in and out of lives that are forever apart.
Above me you sail the sun watery between your thighs,
Chasing the forest birds to the deep eels eyes,
I can always see you knowing I lost your heart.

and now only blurred empty visions of you,
And God only knows where you came to rest,
At the dead end of the white lane where most rest,
Or back to the ocean driftwood bound,
Your heart and the eels making a small desperate sound,
I don't care with my pipe in my cosy musical nest.

Richard Owen Powell

Untitled

First, let the tune
(attending to it's graceful waving arms)
reach out across the room.

And second, let such harmonies and descants
as will come unbidden
to the trembling spine of touch
cascade
like currents under Menai Bridge.

And third,
let all those mysteries
of magic - logic - music
come back to this room
in the light simplicity of love.

Paul Nicholson

13

Homes of England

Streets long endless streets,
Rows of houses stand together,
Braving Englands changing weather.
Surely Wordsworth Milton Keats,
Would see no beauty in those streets,
Those endless streets.

Houses are these the stately homes of England,
In my imagination,
I see the homes of our great nation,
Houses and farms in setting fair,
Where one could breathe a purer air,
In our dear England.

Streets of many houses, homes of England,
But am I wrong, is beauty there,
Can beauty live without fresh air,
Let no grim destiny unforeseen,
Deny us of our lovely green,
Pastures of England.

Phyllis M Lloyd

14

Beyond a Distance View

You I hold
Shake, shake, shake
Wake, wake, wake -
Wake up to time
There is no future
For one who sleeps
Live lives -
It doesn't die,
The world moves,
Doesn't stand still.
There is no future
For one who stands
The future is all
For those who run,
For those who see
An outside world
And realise life
Beyond a distance view.

Ruth Lander

Fertilization

I have blown all thoughts away - to minimize
My mind to some strange science, reduced all
To nothing, and microscopic eyed have tried
To analyse -
And smaller even, over-turned the leaf
And seen Mr Ant, whose life is brief
Cased in, and whose days are droned away
In received belief -
He can't see far, his pride directs his intellect
To matter less, and matter same which like him
Crowds this patch of land, minds matched in
Possessive insect;

and I can't fit in miniature -
My impotent tongue licks lame the air,
Whilst Eden's ghosts amongst the dying daffodils
Are breathing, that Paradise was lost, a nation
Has erred and shamed itself to dust,
And we can't articulate a new creation;

So now my original apples eye,
Renders the air
Thick with yellow scent, and bare,
We slither here -
Our snake - like skin and green tongues flicker;
We writhe, instinctively,
Towards a place where the Red Hearts open,
And flesh can think;
And fertilize.

Karen Mason

White World

Not long ago snow wrapped the fields
In sheets of spotless white
Like ghosts the snow cupped winter trees
Swayed in the winter night.
Like lace the snow festooned the edge
Of eerie wall and fence and hedge

Carpeted white the meadows lie with daisies overlaid
The pear tree and the cherry stand
In robes of white arrayed
And lace of hawthorns hangs today
On hedge where the snowfall lay

Timmy Bach

Brief Encounter

Burnt almond was the colour of her voice
Her eyes were overlarge
as if such detail mattered
and she chattered
wildly
as her fingers searched
inside my shirt.
She loved the feel of hair
'Love-ease' she said was there.
No bra' she wore
and in that shadowy door
in fallows have
we squirmed together
Two lob-worms on one hook
she had that something!
Heavy breathing!
'Saint in torment' look
But when I mentioned bed
She fled!

R Mainwaring

Tribute to Freddie Mercury

Little soldier struggles on. White Queen yawns.
She waits to take the Black Knight. She has no time for pawns.
The struggle is the constant on the ever changing board.
Light and darkness, white and black, little pawn and Lord.

The warrior, his head held high, has reached the farthest side.
And faced her, white and waiting like a wedding-weary bride.
And she is gone, A new Black Queen holds sway over the board.
His march is one of triumph! The little pawn is Lord!

Far beyond and long away
They speak of his courageous play.
'But without meaning to deride -
He's still a little pawn inside'.

The board is tucked away at last, the great Black Queen has lost.
When 'Checkmate' came he heard it from inside the pieces' box.
The strong one had been humbled, yet glories in this claim -
The winner is the little pawn whose soul is in the game.

Anna M K Jones

The Black Mountain

Scarped against the sky it rises it's
Shadow bare of grass and gorse,
Barren are it's granite ledges, worn
Fine through erosive force.
Shrouded in the firmament it's peak
Lies cold and stark,
A tomb for scoria and fossils, from
An age that has left it's mark.
Towering these weathered crags reign
Obscurely above the earth -
A lonely black mountain, sterile since
It's birth.

Donald Sainsbury

Random Memories

Have you ever climbed a mountain in the middle of the night
Sat and watched the new moon rising, sending down it's silver light
On the lakes, and on the rivers, and the valley far below
Leaving half the mount in blackness, and the rest in magic glow.

Have you ever walked in sunshine to a small, secluded cove
Stood and watched the tide returning, heard the pebbles loudly move.
Felt the wind and spray around you, seen the waters looming high -
Crashing on the nearby rocks, and heard the sand grains softly sigh.

Have you ever, in the summer, quietly lain in meadow grass
Watched the grasshopper make music, seen the beetles scurrying past
Heard the bees forever buzzing, working hard throughout the hours,
While a butterfly is landing on the newly opened flowers.

Have you ever walked through woodlands at the turning of the year
Under trees in glorious colour, watched the foxes and the deer.
Seen the colours of the maples, - golden, orange, deepest red,
While the fallen leaves beneath you crack and rustle as you tread.

Have you ever, in the winter, crunched on newly fallen snow,
Felt the soft kiss of the snowflakes, toes and fingers all aglow.
Have you looked through frosted window on a garden glistening
white
Trees and bushes all transfigured in the silence of the night.

Mair Alexander

Compassion

Have you heard the word compassion
Said the wise man to the fool
I doubt you know the meaning
If you never went to school.
The fool, he started crying
And the wise man walked away
A simpleton, the fools best friend
Said, come, you'll be ok.

Norma Phillips

In Secret Dark

If I cannot love outright
in light for all to view,
I'll take my lovers, fond and few
at night, in secret dark
I'll be a park of solace, and in my burnished hollow
sooth his face of sorrow
Whispering - 'Still. Be still'
as with each layer
He discards his daylight wear and lies beside
resigned from care.

Come
Conceive
Cleave out the stars
To light our hallowed grove
With slightest touch our match will catch
And bellowed flame will rise to roaring heights
To mellow
Moonlit thighs

Embrace
Encase
In crescent fast
Past - future - cease to be
Desire is the essence
Of spirituality

And as he sighs to daily toil, the spoils
all mine, Ill bring
Beneath my sheets of down - to sleep
the sleep of rapture drowned
From dawn to twilight - sound.

Sylvie Morgan Hopkin

The Shepherd

The earth is sleeping,
Cold is the night, black as an abysmal cave,
The trees are weeping
Rich blossoms, heavy with scent splashed in April rain.

the open gate creaks,
And shows beyond new earth freshly sown with grain,
The darkest cloud breaks,
Lighting a silent world caught in the mesh of spring.

Primrose droops it's head,
Couching, unseen, amid the trampled grass,
Song of bird has fled,
Only the stream murmurs it's nocturne songs,
Tardy winter lingers,
Trees shiver neath the cold caressing wind,
The shepherd fingers his staff,
Lonely guardian of the night.
His flock lie sleeping,
No terrors of the dark disturb their slumbers,
Woolly heads dreaming,
Of sweet mountain grass washed with the dew of spring.

D Mervyn Jones

Night

Night,
Darkness, Wrapped
in a gossamer shawl.

shadows
slinky,
short,
tall
fall
from the houses,
caught
by the alley's

Reaching out,
hiding in,
Corners black as silk.
Deadly
as a word.

Ann Eyton Jones

Where Cars Cannot Come

Where cars cannot come
Is where I would go;
Away from the drum
Of their cyclic agenda
So you cannot remember
The vision you know.

I walk off the highways
And into the lanes;
To recall the memories
With wind my companion
With sun as my champion
To listen to all, of natures refrains.

The rustle of long grass,
The wild whining trees,
A tune, on the edge of glass
Strikes the first chord,
A bloodthirsty sword.
To deep in the wood now, for any reprieve.

A flash of the sun
On the edge of the water,
Like the startling fun
Contained in her smile
And roasted by guile
I saw, Neptunes daughter.

I cannot go on now,
Where cars cannot come,
But I renew the vow
To do what is needed
And quietly unheeded
I take out the gun.

For of all that is troubling me
This now is the sum,
That a sound greater, considerably,
Reside in this lane
And nothing exists, to blot out it's pain;
Where cars cannot come,
...Is my heart
...Is my brain.

Cyril Jones

Untitled

Embracing greed and tremble
a life to throw away.
My trust in human nature
has this day gone astray.

A burdened life that withers
withholding all to gain.
Deceptive peace to live on
and suffer secluded pain.

Pursued by clouded visions
of unguarded riches lay.
Hoarding all emotions
that claim their lives away.

Deceit and lust rules merry
depriving gracious peace.
When faced with true emotions
they bow their heads in ease.

Devoid of earthly pleasures
where greed does well to win.
A human soul unfeeling
was this day claimed by sin.

Mansel

A Welsh Spring

That day,
slate skies still gloomed
the slanting fields,
but timid pink smiled faintly
between the clouds.

Grave sheep,
catched to the hill's green cant,
stirred in the mellowing air,
and misty pastures, corsetted
by cattle-keeping walls,
appeared to meditate
upon their coming colours.

Deep in the valley's throat
a tipsy tractor undulated,
loudly blue, defiant
against the earth's brown quiet.

Suddenly,
a whirr of pigeons
in arrowed flight,
climbed then dived
into the valley's side,
melting in the solvency of trees
like the easing of a pain.

Rubber-shod
I trod the meadow's ooze,
feeling the muscling turf
beneath my feet; then,
welcoming the simplifying air,
I took my first firm step
from the winter of your going.
Vic Rees

Contentment

Encrusted all the window panes
With threads of trembling light
And nude trees outside are clothed
With garments gleaming bright
But in my room brisk firelight
Casts shadows on the walls.
And to my hand all books I love
And their beauty calls.

Glenys Thomas

What Would it be Like if ...?

What would it be life if
Stone age man saw planes
Fighters, low and noisy
Buzzing the weather vanes.
Weather vanes?

Showing the points of the compass
North South West and East
No, you cannot eat it
Nor is it a kind of beast.
Compass?

It shows you where you're going
It points to where you've been
It works by magnetism
Which is something never seen.
Magnetism?

If I can't explain a weather vane
To a man from years gone by
I haven't got the slightest chance
Of telling how planes fly.

Judith Pettit

Almost Lost

What can you do for me dear Lord?
I'm weary, and I've lost my way
I remember the time I walked closely with you
But I've changed such a lot since that day.

I'm drinking, and swearing, and I never pray
Have no patience, don't care what I say
But I know in my heart, that I've strayed from you Lord
Why is Satan having his way?

Your book lying there is covered with dust
Reflecting my soul, beginning to rust
The company I keep can be no ones desire
Should be much better, and so much higher.

In a moment of weakness, I strayed from you Lord
And followed the crowd on that day
How I wish I'd been stronger, and stayed by your side
For you are the life and the way.

Oh, draw me back Saviour, and forgive all my sin
I'm the sheep that wandered astray
Take me back in your fold, and let me begin
To love you again from this day.

John Hugh Jones

Hell Play

A card pulled out of some old dusty pack.
Placed face down on a biting hot slab.
Faded with the yellow of age.
I turn it over - the ace of spades.

Facing me a strangers mask.
I hesitate, and then I ask,
'Why do you stare in that strange way?'
The stranger smiles and whispers 'play'

A scream in the distance, the cry of a child.
The tapping of hoofs on hot cracked tiles.
My head is throbbing with the dull ache of fear.
The sound of a nightmare whispering in my ear.

The stranger cackles a dry scorched sound.
Rakes his hoofs across smouldering ground.
Reaches out with a gnarled withered hand,
Whispers softly, 'you do understand'

'You're in hell and there's no way out,
Don't ever try to scream or shout.
You are here because you were destined to be,
In my kingdom of flames and ecstasy'.

Regan Ashurst

The Colour of Silence

The flames of twilight wane
Into ashes of darkness
Transformation begins.....
Freezing temperature drops and drops,
Whispering wind
Winds its way - between misty valleys,
Over reclining hills and jagged mountains.

Magical symbols of heaven descend,
Dampening cold, clear window panes,
Silently drifting and covering.
A new world will soon appear.

Silence is concluded by
Hovering and soaring creations of the sky.
Rekindled twilight flames emerge
Relighting the stage.
White is the colour of silence.
Joyful, infant faces agree.

David Jones

The Pattern of Life

As one life ends, another begins
And some folk grieve, others rejoice
The pattern of life goes on ......

A last breath grasped, tired eyes close
No more pain or suffering
A full life lived, now ending
The pattern of life goes on ......

A first breath gasped, eyes unfolding
The first taste of air, lungs filling
A new life starting its living
The pattern of life goes on ......

Sympathy flowers, tears of sadness.
Congratulating messages, elated gladness
The pattern of life goes on and on ......

Sally Moreton

Untitled

Dressed in black leather from head to toe.
Gleaming great steed, waiting to go.
Easy at first, then a mighty roar
The powerful motor bike speeds from the door.
A quick wave of the hand, a kiss blown on the wind.
He's gone from my sight, but not from my mind.
Into the traffic, along the main road.
Death was his passenger, Death was his load.
Weaving and turning, a rush to get there.
A glance at the time, then a gasp of despair.
If only you'd waited, if only you'd stayed.
For only a minute, for only a shade.
Then I wouldn't be here, tending your grave.

Joan Littlehales

Nursery Rhyme

Ring-a-ring of funeral bells
Throw the pussies down the wells
Ninety people fell and drowned
When London bridge came falling down

Ba-ba black sheep's locked outside
Now the farm's gone apartheid
Today's pressures just too much
Humpty Dumpty's cracking up

Jack Horner rings the Sunday Times
Utters a few warning lines
Slams down receiver then he's gone
Sticks in a thumb explodes a bomb

Sitting drinking ginger ale
Duke of York turns ghostly pale
Ten thousand men go up in smoke
Their ashes settle round his cloak

Mary Mary quite contrary
Jumps from the eleventh story
Meets the pavement face to face
But makes an impact on that place

Pavement artist then takes part
Makes Mary Mary objects d'art
Splattered stone stands in the Tate
With Mary Mary on a plate

Sing a song of 50p
Mummy say one more to me
No more no more good night good night
God reaching down turns off the light.

Kevin Brewer

Nocturne

Nice to have a corner of the house
given over to something that comes
and goes
access to some nocturnal familiar
be it cat, bat, or owl

Through flap, gap, vent, via secret way
homing with coded messages, beyond words,
beyond reason,
smelling of the night and flight
vibrant with cool trajectories

Fur or feather to brush the dream's outline
as it traces the alignments of the dawn house
as night wine yields to morning milk
and its emissaries seek crevice, nook, or cushion

Martin Hibbert

39

If I Painted My Life

If I painted my life, it would mostly be grey.
With rare flames of scarlet for each special day
And the odd strand of silver where I kept my illusions
Mixed in with the blues, marking times of confusion.

If I painted my life there'd be cloudbursts and storms
For the days when I gave up and agreed to conform
And then I'd paint stars one for each dream
That gave life a meaning, or so it once seemed.

If I painted my life then the beautiful days
Would shimmer in gold and light up the greys
And your soul would be drawn to the soft glowing lights
Where the splashes of gold tell of our shared nights.

Beverley Hill

Cold Blood

They crossed in cleric's collars as daybreak sidled in
Bearing altar candles and a panoply of sin.
They made covert communion, hunched like cellar rats
Breathing terrors incense, sieving death from molten wax.
Beneath a high-rise Temple where concrete caged the light
They buried desecration in an obscene, furtive rite.

Sing rebel songs to greet them
For no matter what they do
Provisionals are heroes
Their cause is just and true.

She drifted through the drizzle in an evening gown of jade
Enchanted by the echoes of First Night accolade.
She was innocent of malice, bigotry or spite.
Bright-eyed and golden headed, savouring the night.
Street-neon lined her beauty, making jewel-strings of the rain
The fireball slashed her, shrieking, in a razor-blaze of pain.

Pluck glass shards from her eyeballs
Rinse her cold blood from the dust
Then ask her bereft parents
If the cause is true or just.

Roger Jones

41

The Workmen

The workmen were in the High Street
Gazing at a hole.
The tarmac opening caverns
Of faults and queries to be exposed.
Black coated they stood together
Huddled and bent in thought
Pick axe at the ready
Spades and rubble,
Soil and errors to be sought..
But were they in a rugby scrum
Or plotting a spryish plot?-
Or were they whispering some
Lecherous candid thoughts
About a passing piece of skirt?

Joan Richardson

Soldier Boys

Marching
In time
Eyes front ... shoulders back
Young boys
Soldier boys
Marching ...
Off to war.

Fighting
Bullets fly
Blood flows ... poppy red
Young boys
Soldier boys
Marching ...
Into war.

Exhausted
Battletorn
Valiant still .... giving more
Young boys
Soldier boys
Dying ...
This, is war.

Ghostly
Marching on
Thousands more ... at Heaven's Gate
Tell us then
Young boys Soldier boys

What is it all for?

Pam Probert

The Poet

A poet should not
work for his bread.

He should be one
with his own self, a whole
and perfect being.

He should hear the grass grow,
the squirrel turn
the nut in his hands,
the earthworm tremble.
He should not hazard his Muse.

A poet should be fed by the people.
If he wants more than bread,
shoot him.

Herbert Williams

A Letter to Paul on His Tenth Birthday

My Dearest Paul,
I can't believe
It's ten long years
Since you arrived upon this earth.
Your father phoned,
Excitedly,
To us in Rhyl,
To let us know of your safe birth.
We drank champagne
To celebrate
This first-born child
A new branch on our family tree.
We've watched you grow
From screaming babe
To whining tot:
You worried us incessantly!
But Paul, my dear,
You have become
All that we hoped:
A loving, caring, happy boy.
On your big day
We wish you health;
We wish you wealth;
God's blessing for a life of joy.

Kathleen Wendy Jones

A Fine Day in April

The sea so flat and calm
with hardly a ripple,
and a hazy blue sky.

No ships or sails in sight.
Just two seabirds,
Dipping, diving, disappearing into the mist.

The winds of March,
Mixed with April showers,
Give way to a warm Spring.

Two ladies sitting in the shelter,
Chattering, looking, pointing.
A little old man walks his dog.

Three small children
Take Father for a paddle,
His trousers rolled up to the knee.

People busy walking to and fro,
Midst all the shops with 'sales',
Nowhere to park the car this day.

The pier reaching out
As far as the eye can see,
That's Llandudno by the sea.

Jeannie O'Neill

Wonder Woman

A daughter, a sister, a wife, and a mother
lived in the same house, and had the same lover,
slept in the same bed, under the same roof
If you don't believe me I'll give you some proof,
They all had four children, making it six
there is no mystery, there are no tricks,
The daughter, sister, wife and mother, you see
All are the same person, yes you've guessed it, it's me,
For I am the daughter to my mother
and I am the sister to my brother,
I am the wife to my lover
and of course, I'm my children's mother.

Jean Mary Perkins

Pagan

Once you spoke my name aloud,
You raised your voice and stood up proud.
But then they came, and cast aside
All other faiths, you chose to hide.
In feeble whispers did you preach
The doctrines that I bade you teach.
You left me in my hour of need
To fight alone, you watched me bleed.
And yet your silence still you kept,
You showed no shame, you never wept;
And now you beg to me for aid,
The one you served and then betrayed.
Pray to their God, who gave his Son
In the name of love, as you have done.
You cursed my name, renounced your vows:
I hold you as a Christian now.

Julie Ann Lake

To Fly Free

Look down you mountains tall, do you recall
The desolation wrought in our forefather's time,
The rape of our green valley, exposing the black wealth
That many men and many lived did again.
The mighty mechanical monsters munched their way
Into our lives, condemning us to a polluted future,
A black horizon.
Born in the shadow of the slag heaps,
A career carved in coal, a burrowing mole,
Moving from the soft air of the early morning
To a stifling, inky darkness, a remoteness in black earth;
Digging out those symbols of hardship, worry, and of pain.
That urge, that longing to be in open air, to fly free,
O'erwhelmed us again and again.

Now look once more, black turns to green.
The winding gear is still. The railway lines
Are rusted, twisted, gone.
No more the mindless toil, the rise and shine,
The hob-nailed boots of our mining infantry, echoing
Along the terrace streets.
The scars will fade upon your mottled slopes,
The verdant grass return along your valley side.
Redundant, each man looks for a new life now,
Far from those depths of nothingness. And us,
Too late for us a new life beckons. For we lie
At rest beneath the very soil we sought to excavate.
Our struggle is over, our efforts unrewarded.
But our proud spirits soar above you.

In open air, at last, we fly free.

Pat Davies

49

A Dyfed Forest

I stood in the forest and looked around
I listened - quite still - but little sound
Tall pine trees reached upward, towards the sky
Silence was broken, I heard a gull cry.
Then standing on springy needles of larch
Lying there since Autumn - now it is March.
Damp perfume from pine trees wafted all round
Then close by a tree some fresh moss I found.
Deep in the forest 'twas really dark
A squirrel'd been here he'd left his mark
Some bark was well scratched, and nut shells were there

But he wasn't visible anywhere.
But thousands of eyes were looking at me
I felt their presence near every tree.
But when it is dark I expect they'll come out
Sniffing and hunting and playing about
Rabbit and fox and a mouse or rat
Weasel and badger and perhaps a polecat.
The secret night life of the forest scene..
And they will all know where we have been.

Wendy Dedicott

Untitled

Swansea docks grey in the space
Between the sky and the wasted earth,
Scarred by quarrying; as though man's frantic passions
Have taken refuge in the labyrinths beneath.

So we stand above on windswept ground,
Staring emptiness about with nothing to show
For our possible feelings, whilst uncertain pasts,
Wrestle for light in the darkness below.

Michael Haynes

Remembrance Sunday

Fields strewn with poppies,
Like tear stained 'kerchiefs -
Rows of bleach-white stones
March where bodies lie.
High-reaching unmarked tomb
Below lies unknown loved men,
All these are the spoils
And booty from the war.

Widows robed in weeping reeds,
Orphans, homeless alone.
Coffins, photographs and poppies
Are all that now remains.
Memories left to haunt dulled minds
Are pinned like medallion hearts;
All these are the spoils
And booty from the war.

Dawn Davies

New Year

The year is ending
As it always ends
Rejoice and forget your sins;
The rain is falling
As it always falls,
And the sea comes rolling in.

The sun is rising
As it always rises.
Unfold the new year plan;
The wind is blowing
As it always blows
Fresh hope from man to man.

Alan Dickson

Contemplating the Statue of Dylan Thomas in the Swansea Marina

O master craftsman
harnessed to the earth
in cobblestoned court
As a wilderness of words in the silent sea
maroons you in maritime melancholy.

O learned sculptor
blankness ever looms
without rhyme or voice
But the fitful inventions of a restless pen
have wrought such great feats in the long lives of man.

O bard eternal
the incoming tide
drowns with loud acclaim
As a covenant of waves from the deafening deep
pours forth to extol the live soul rocked in sleep.

Sylvia Williams

The Scars Still Remain

The air was cold with baited breath
As he realised he had caused her death
He loved his wife with all his heart
He remembered the words, 'till death do us part'

But he wasn't to blame for the end of her life
It was a drunken driver who killed his wife
But he carried the burden at the scene of the crime
And the scars still remain after all of this time

They had gone for a walk to get some fresh air
The car came from nowhere, it just isn't fair
He stands by her graveside each day of his life
Remembering times he had spent with his wife

The driver is free now to do what he chooses
All he remembers are his cuts and bruises
He doesn't remember he took someone's life
That night in the past, when he killed a man's wife.

Jason Bannan

Time

Time, an unseen sculptor carving mountains into the rugged shapes
that inspire men to new heights.

Time, silently moulding the rolling hills, diligently chiselling
the paths of a thousand rivers, leading to the cryptic sea,
whose coasts have been fashioned by time's invisible hand and the
seas breaking white fingers.
Time ticks on.
Time as a craftsman can create
Time as a vandal can destroy.
It crushes the hopes of all people, and like a thief it steals the dreams
of everyone
In advance of time is hope and worry,
Following time is relief or sadness, each one striking at different
times.
Once they come all the hope and worry are forgotten
Time ticks on.
No one can master time as they can master people.
When these people are dust time ticks on.
Time is a more powerful ruler than any king.
Time controls people, runs their lives and drives them to their
graves.
Time cannot be harnessed by people but time harness's people.
And when all is said and done time ticks on.

Robert Temple Stroud

The Mountain

Each day you'll find her without fail,
Peeking through her misty veil,
Bathing in the morning dew,
At her feet heather grew.
I've tasted the stream so cool and clear,
Like a ribbon that flows down to the sea.
Tiny lambs fleecy and white,
Casting shadows at twilight.
Whispering winds what tales they tell,
To this ageless beauty who guards them well.
The air around her fresh and clean,
A snow tipped hat, a dress of green.
For gracious lady she'll remain,
I'll be back to visit once again.

Joyce D Morris

Time for Action

Where lies the dormant spark to
Ignite
the drudgery of this day?
Endless passing hours
Merge so much in conspiracy.
Swallowed hours reveal a need
To moisten this dry throat,
Too numb for cries.

A radio tinkles across the way,
Melodies allow mental mastication,
Ceaselessly through the day.
I sit in this vacuum of experience
Untouched by wind or speech or inspiration.
How I long for a change
From this natural stasis.

Like the cell-man
I strike off days;
Dreading the end.
For I will be punished
When the scales fall
Against me.
A wanton misuse of the mortal clock.

Martin Griffiths

Dreams

Dreams, dreams of yesterday,
all the past failings and hurts,
all of the people who've come and gone,
all the mistakes left unfixed.

Dreams, dreams of fantasy,
of heroes, villains and maidens,
of all the right cues and right words,
where all but yourself can lose.

Dreams, dreams of today,
where work is so distant and far away
no knowing what you've done that day
just switching the mind into auto-pilot.

Dreams, dreams of ecstasy,
where people are naked and very obliging
and your the stud everywhere you go,
never failing to make it.

Dreams, dreams of future,
with all the good things it must hold,
where profits are big and ideas bold
and love and marriage so perfect.

Dreams, dreams of darkness,
of never breathing, never seeing,
where death is uncertain, frightening
and dreams are oh so cold.

John-James T Nisbet

Henry Vaughan

Though the last fragments of his well-worn bones have
Long since spread through the soil of his loved land;
The swarthy cells may not be seen in root or branch
In the yew and ivy which made a bed for his body nor
in the dark silver twigs of hedges that line the lanes he walked.

Today I saw them, etched against an evening star bright sky.
He knows serenity now, bright certainty
The star he knew and held in view all through the brief night
Now holds him close, enfolds him, in ever-lasting day
He is not lost, the small still Silurian voice

His words ring anew and are radiant
The sweet scent of his burial flowers lingers
And the mountains still return his calm gaze.

J P Bradnick

Funeral Thoughts

On nights when the moon writes her slow secret messages,
Across the earth's patient pages,
I hear the muted music of sad psalms playing at my passing.

I smell the funeral flowers at my head,
And feel the soft folds of feeble weeping shrouds
Still grieving, as they hide the still cold hands of death.

I hear the soul-sad bell's dark muffled tongue,
Toll as in ancient dreaded days
From listening spires lamenting, mesmerised.

My closed eyes flow a thousand memories paths,
Where friendship's fabric bound the long-linked hands'
And youth's pink feet ran wild and scanty clad.

I hear the distant voices call my name'
And speak of promises forgotten and unkept
While yesterday's secrets lie forgotten on the lawn,

Sad icy swords approach my bed.
Then comes the cold kiss upon my shrunken cheek.
A sudden spasm
And I wake.
Alone
Afraid
But still alive.

Sheila Batten

Morning Dew

The pearls they slowly fade away
From leafy blades from whence they lay
They come at night when no one sees
To be drawn back by morning breeze

Only creatures of the night
See them form before the light
What strange hands have placed them there
With gentleness and loving care

The sun appears and they're all gone
Back to gods where they belong
Drawn high up into open skies
To reign down on our meagre lives

D B Davis

That Deadly Seed of Doubt

Subconsciously devised
ill conceived plot
born of his weakness
creatively developed
like an embryo
enacted as if I were despised.

With bitter-sweet intent
planted it deep inside her
disguised as love
nurtured it grew
while she withered away
so tragically mistakenly meant.

Joy Foster

Our Lodgers

We had lodgers at our house, we did,
John and George and Mick and Sid.
John was old with balding head
Pleased he'd managed not to wed.
Like to sit on the old sea wall,
Got so drunk once he had a fall.
They fished him out and he did say,
Not a drop I'll touch from this day.
George as a lad went to sea,
On a training ship, so it be.
On a training ship, so it be.
Stole a pair of boots when he was eight.
That was the punishment at that date.
Mick was Irish like his name,
Singing in the pubs was his fame.
Courted a girl who went into the church,
Became a Nun, he was left in the lurch.
Last but not least we come to Sid,
Always caused trouble, was what he did,
The Police would be 'round knocking the door,
As Grannie would pick him up from the floor.
You're not staying here any more, she would say
'I'll be glad when they come to take you away.'

They died of course, one by one
For Mick a wake was good fun,
George in a sack went to sea,
John said a whiskey case for me.
Sid the worst was the last
Fighting to the end as was his past.
Of course grannie outlived them all
They were happy times I do recall.

Caril Krane

Dylan

Throw me, drunk as a lord on this park bench,
Throw me, lightly as a ball to high heaven,
Silver-strung by umbilical cord to low earth,
That I may heavily fall among the fern on the hill.
Keep tight the straining string in giant-hand,
And guide my devious descent to my lonely covert,
There, sprawled, cushioned and fancy free,
To stretch my alcoholic - rivened limbs,
I shall drowsily dream as always
Of boyhood's foal-like scamperings,
Youth's droolings beneath the moon,
And the glowering, latent dominion of death.

Roy Morgan

In your Absence

Afterwards
I raise my head;
the words I needed flow,
my mind no longer spinning from the blow.

All I gave you, you refused,
or you abused, or -
yes, the word I'm coming to is 'used'.

'A hen party', you said,
but wore your lovebird plumage
and left me to languish in the cage.
You said you'd be in late and tight, that night,
but returned and dragged me into bed instead,
to slake, not lust,
but rage.

You were having your revenge on someone:
I lay awake, and ached inside,
and wondered who;
but it was only when you told me that I knew,
by which time it wasn't any use.
You walked out on me for him
and called me weak,
and used my silence and my tears as your excuse.

Only in your absence
can I give my point of view,
but in your presence
I could live with that,
forgive you that;
it's nothing new.

Chris Poote

Another Dawn

Take each day as it comes, joyfully.
A fresh challenge, a new situation.
Unique, so special, so precious;
The wealth of each day is the experience
it brings,
Broadened understanding,
deeper insights.
Preconceptions shattered,
daydreams awakened.
As clay in the potter's hands,
shaped by the imprints of life.
What beauty is the potter making?
What shape goes into the kiln?
Remain agile in your thinking,
Ready to leap like an athlete over hurdles
of reasoning.
Complexities simplified,
simplicities scrutinized.
As the sunset approaches,
so comes another dawn.

Trystan Wyn Davies

Dragonfly

A month to live while on the wing,
A month to find a mate and wed,
Then lay your eggs in wayside pool,
A month to live and then you're dead.

Hunting above the stagnant water,
Perching on pond-side green-leaved weed
With wings outspread on long, blue body -
A hawk among sparrows you are indeed.

F W Hibbert

A Day in the Life

Sitting alone in the throes of the winter,
Whispering words that died with the sun,
Staring with eyes that are stinging and bitter,
Crying inside, for the music has gone.

Walking alone in the curve of the coastline,
Cursing the demon that murdered the fire,
Cold as the heart that is dying inside him,
Mad as the heart that gave birth to the liar.

Standing alone in the kingdom of tears,
Watching for life through the knives of the rain,
Dying in memory, silently waiting,
Hate for himself growing strong with the pain.

Leaving along, left alone in the storm
By a dove disillusioned by silence and stone.
Racing through crashing night, chased by a man
Who will always be spurned, who will never be home.

Ceri Stafford

Detritus

There in that cluttered curtained room
amongst the depressing ruins of their lives
wondering was there a special name
for the dust which falls out of woodworm holes
she came across that strange pleading note
written by him but oddly never given to her.
Listening to her mind reading it she wanted to cry.
If only he had come to her with those words
how different everything might have worked out.
Turning the paper over she was surprised
to find it addressed to another woman.

John Adrian

The Rose

Petals as soft as a baby's skin
Envelope the delicate heart within
Suns rays shine on your perfect form
And disperse the dew left by the dawn
Behind your thorn you shy away
Upon your leaves your head does lay
Your beauty, above all others towers
You truly are the queen of flowers.

Janice Burge

Our Bond

We can't touch it
But feel it.
Just as I felt the pain of the bruises
I collected on your behalf.
I gave you a few too if I remember rightly,
But no-one else could or dare!
Protecting you from all dangers
Was the role I elected to play.
(And the feeling is still the same today.)
Do you know I can still vividly recall
Your hand in mine
As I safely guided you to the school gates.
(You know, your hand was bigger than mine even then.)
I remember the fear I felt
When watching you swim way out of your depth
And the way you'd laugh when I called you back.
I guess I must have been a pain
To you
And your friends.
(In fact, many times I saw the look of impatience and lack of under-
standing on your face.)
We still can't touch it
But know it'll always be our bond,
This strange and beautiful sisterly love.

Sonja Burton

Dawn

When night to the day is led
And the light from the rushing moon is shed
Beyond the winter pale,
The faded skin to amber turns,
That strip of sky that dawning burns
The hoarfrost dry.

Paul Williams

Untitled

As I wander through the woods
Not a creature do I see,
All is quiet all is still
I feel that eyes are watching me

Could there be
A snake in the grass,
Watching me, with fervent eyes' as I pass,

Sunlight shining
Through the trees,
Branches creaking
In the breeze,

The grass is damp
With the morning dew,
Woodland flowers bloom,
With buds anew.

Be careful!
Where you tread,
For where you place your foot
Could that not be someone's bed.

William A Stowe

Sheep

Last week I looked quite pretty but now I look a sight,
If I hadn't had my hair cut it would have been alright,
The other girls had their's cut it was a mass event,
Supposedly for our own good infestation to prevent,
The boys as well were taken in their crowns in glory shed,
I'm sure they feel embarrassed though their faces don't look red,
The lot of us were rounded up it's something that we fear,
It's happened to us more than once it happens every year,
Another thing they do to us I'd like you all to know,
They make us take an awful bath we line up in a row,
We cannot write to our MP's our silence we must keep,
No notice would they take of us - because we're only sheep.

Norma McKerracher

Rain

It rained last night, what a lovely sound,
With kisses so welcome, it softened the ground.
A raindrop sparkles on a leaf by my door
Iridescent and trembling waiting for more.
A spiders web shimmers, gossamer lace.
With fairy like fingers it caresses my face.
A snail leaves a trail as it moves slowly along
The rain freshened air fills with the birds lovely song.
The world is awakening, the sun will arise
Flame coloured banners will colour the skies,
New buds will open and flowers bloom again
Welcoming new life, brought by Gods blessing of rain.

Winifred Grace Turner

The Beginning of the End

And what is left for me now?
What must I do tomorrow?
Will I see the dawn of another endless day?
Can I face the grief and the sorrow?
Must I journey on through life
Treading steps to nowhere?
Give me a reason for living
Or a burden of sorrow to bear
Wounded heart, stop bleeding!
Aching tears, cease to roll!
Agony chimes loud in my ear
Like a ceaseless death roll
I crawl on my knees,
My hands searching for death
Because, without you, there is no life -
No life worth living
No love worth taking,
No love worth giving.
Dusty are my feet
As I tread the unending path of fear and darkness,
No light to see, because
No light hath enough
To light my path.
Death, come soon.

Brenda Thomas

The Greatest Love

Deep within her marble vault
The bride sleeps
Her face cold, as her stone prison.
Dreaming pictures of Antony
The man?.... the soldier
Fought wars of words
That burn deeper
than the cutting edge.
She lay
with serpent close,
to Antony's shrine
a serpent crowned,
sole sovereign of the world
Built in Nilus' land
or the city where gladiator
meets gladiator
striking steel to stone.
Like him
who gave himself
to flesh of mine, in bond
and like stony walls, smashed down
Fragmented
Turning false amity to hate
But now?
He sleeps on stygian shore.
The cause a sovereign war?
or the love of a Penthesilea.
But two hearts lie entained.
United together
by Tiber's snake.

Rachael Thomas

Swalk

Seal my lips
With your kisses,
Warm me
with your embrace.
Make me tremble
in your arms.
Let me shiver
at your touch.
Hold me close,
never leave me.
Love me with
a burning rage.
Feel the beat
of my heart,
as I scream
your name
in yearning.

Catherine Ann Keohane

Liberty

Oh what delight
This liberty
Setting in flight
Minds imagery
Searching the wind
For sound unseen,
Soaring to find
Joy bursting green,
Though gnarled boughs bare
Their leaves have shed
And windswept air
Mourns overhead.
While through dark day
In fear men grope
Where cruel decay
Blights mortal hope.
Oh what delight
That soul may be
Set free in flight
With imagery.
And inward eye
With beauty blest
Reveal lifes peace
And gentleness.

E W Ray

Taff

We met again last Friday when I brought
Eggs. You hobbled up to say Hello; your coat
Was soft and good although the legs were stiff
And the eyes marbled: dear, kind, old dog.
Now it is Wednesday; the vet has been
And you are gone but not with fallen cows
And death-wish ewes. The man who loved you knows
A cloven rock high on the mountain side,
Where he reviews the borders of his realm;
He put there with boulders on the top.
Only stones, Preseli skies and buzzards
Are above. I'm glad we met again so lately,
If just to say Hello that was goodbye.

Marianne Whitelaw

Cardboard City

Night after night they lay their heads
In the cardboards city.
With nowhere else to make their home
It's such a tragic pity.

Wandering around the streets
Looking for a crust,
They must be careful who they meet
There's no one they can trust.

For whatever reason they are in this situation
They find themselves with lost pride
And total desolation.

Up and down the streets they go
Sometimes on their own,
Looking for a better place
And somewhere to call home.

Jim Henderson

Too Much Independence

Too much independence creates strife
There must be special times, to reach
out and touch the one you love, you must.
There must be times to share,
To talk
To care
To smile,
To walk
To cry
To love,
Just for awhile
too much independence can destroy
Barriers come up, which annoys,
Loneliness intrudes, causing suffering
and pain,
This brings no joy to the independence
game.

Hope Roberts

Clean Vision

Our minds awash with dirty linen of TV soaps
Imagined lives of make-believe hopes.
Daily living, the struggle to survive
Stressful needs, children's wants come alive
Enough food on the table, head above water by a
nose
Telephone bills, mortgage rises, expensive clothes
A drink in the pub, a stroll in the park
GTI Golf roars past. It's made its mark.
Material dreams of things to come
Life's price is to be paid, the total sum
For what we see from our screened vision
Is the bubbles fancy from the television.

Terence Sancho

Pensarn Beach

Sitting in the car
Beneath the May moon, as it creeps
Across the velvet star studded sky.
The beach dappled in creeping gold
The stones silent beneath the wheels.
You in my arms speaking soft
Mesmerising murmurs.
My heads heady with your words
Of love, like good wine.
Golden moments in a gold tinged world.
Lights flicker in the distant depths
Like a thousand glow worms,
Out for their evening stroll.
The scent of your skin and the
Tantalising touch of your fingers
On my body, playing a delicate time
Better than any virtuoso.
I am your instrument, and you play me.
Your composition of words and touch.
Is this love, or is this heaven?
Perhaps the two are one.

Arnold Austin Roberts

The Tides of Love

The tides of love wash over me.
Threatening to drag me away,
But I cling to the debris of sanity
To keep me from going astray.

Frightened of drowning in passion,
Yet afraid that I'll miss the tide,
I play in the shadows pretending to swim,
So I can be at your side

Karen Brown

Beauty and Peace

Bleached rocks
Under the burning sun
Dolphins and turtles
Made with wet sand

Sky blue waves
Trimmed with white lace
Stroke firmly my body
And gently caress my face

I gaze into the blue sea
The blue skies laced
With see through white clouds
Their beauty fills my soul

My hungry and thirsty soul
hungry for beauty and peace
A peace and beauty unknown to most
But longed by all.

Makis Lazos

When the Mist Clears

A mass of clinging entrapment
graces the drifting storm
in a conspiracy of eeriness
on a cloudy day.
Frozen faces upturned to the waves;
voyagers threadbare
discussing ways and means;
bold an evil drifting on the tide,
It is rumoured in these parts
that gold-heavy galleons
vanish in the sun
when the mist clears.

Donna Menadue

Collector's Piece

Like a piece of fine porcelain
you took me
off the shelf
and place me
on display
for all the world to see:
An ornament
to your good taste;
acquired
at a price;
to be handled
lovingly
- but not often.

Like a piece of flawed porcelain
you left me
on the shelf
and replace me
thrown away
with no-one there to see:
shattering
like my dreams;
imperceptibly
when I found
you are not
a connoisseur
- but a collector.

Lyndsay Joan Waymont

Phobias and Allergy

Have you heard about poor Ernie, the claustrophobic worm?
Thoughts of dark and closed in places, really make his stomach churn.
And poor old Percy Sparrow, he really got a fright when he hatched
out in a tree top - he just couldn't stand the height!
Not forgetting Henry the Herring, well, he tried but couldn't swim.
If he doesn't get some lessons soon - he may end up in a tin.
But, here in Wales, there is a sheep, who finds life *very* dull
he has to walk round in his 'undies' *Cos he's allergic to the wool'*.

Norma C Crone

Barber

Three miles walk for a hair-cut,
dad's tongue, whip-like
telling me I'm not tired,
that it isn't much further.

Wil Pendre's hut is held together
with not quite knocked-in-nails
and old Exide battery signs.
I sit on a bum-smooth bench
with tobacco stained old men.

My turn,
I perch on a plank
across the barber's high chair,
eye to eye with Wil.

He knows only one style -
desert campaign, 1944,
Africa.
His big hands on my young neck,
his face so close
I get the alcohol off his breath.

I sit like a brush.
Will has no time for children,
he prefers the heat,
the sand gritting his scissors,
his favourite salon
a well camouflaged tank.

My fringe cut as crooked as possible,
my neck shaved like a pine cone,
I am walked home,
ear lobes
slightly bleeding.

Gwyn Parry

Restless Home

He sits watching from the window
Closed against life and fresh air
The sweetness of a spring breeze
Held out with the reach of memory
As distant as forgotten youth
The old church clock
Ticks out its revenge
Calling hourly invitations
To join past loved ones
To surrender to the eternal slumber
Lifting a work worn hand,
He scratches a rough chin
Feeling the sagging flesh
That was once firm and desirable
He presses the bell for a nurse
Anger surrounds him like a hairy blanket
Lost with memory and youth is dignity
Unable now even to urinate upright
A home from home his daughter said
As she rushed back to her modern semi
To wait for her inheritance
He smiles to others who walk the corridors
Talking of wars fought, and battles won
Walking unseen dogs
Men living to watch each other die
Lifes final cabaret

Margaret Paterson

Autumn Gold

Golden leaves beneath my feet,
Autumn winds through my hair,
Flowers fade in slow retreat,
Foxes sleeping in their lair.

Ashen skies of nimbus flocks,
Shrieking geese flee from the east,
Falling showers of icy drops,
Soaking land, man and beasts.

Short days fly from dawn to dusk,
Chill nights sheltered by crackling fire,
Cattle in byre, fed on husks,
Springs green pastures their desire.

Boughs of apples creak and groan,
hazels hardening on the tree,
Fields of stubble, freshly mown,
Swallows gone beyond the seas.

Orions sword arm held on high,
His flashing belt diamond bright,
The autumn stars invade the sky,
And silvery moon lights up the night.

It's chestnut roasting, marshmallow toasting,
Hot toddies and mulled ales downed,
In the hedgerow robins boasting,
Leafy carpet covers the ground.

Autumn, herald for the winter,
All brown and red burnished gold,
Time is passing like a sprinter,
Now the year is growing old.

William Hayles

My Darkest Hour

I think I must be dead
All be it for the finest threads
To which I so dearly cling,
And has not the light evaded
Mine eyes so veined
While tethered is my ancient tongue.

I think I must be dead
And in languorous mood I contemplate,
For did I not bear witness to my birth?
And in so doing - my death!
Who is 'He' - Who grants us sublime vision?
Only to discard us in the mire
of our own ignorance.

I think I must be dead
Although I have not yet succumbed
To the angels' dirge,
Guiding me forth into the eternal abyss.
Wilt, 'Thou' call my name?
That I might be free to relinquish
The burden of my birth.

Marr Andrew Davies

Thought

I stand alone and gaze
with inner sight upon the range
and see my little cottage on the hills.
The dresser with its willow pattern plates
reminiscent of my childhood days.
Transient, ephemeral, thought moves on
faster than the speed of light,
at times drifting, sparkling and in flight
enriching the spectre of life, then
kindling hopes and expectations to ethereal heights.
Recalling too the friendship and the hardships of our times.
This unique precious gift unequalled on life's page
in this extraordinary age.
Classics, science brightly prosper
with the gift of thought, thus
enabling mankind's aspirations
To its final goal.

J R Williams

Strange People

Some people think it very strange
when ramblers climb the Snowdon range
in weather foul, in snow or hail
and even laugh to tell the tale.

Yet ramblers take it in their stride
to scorn the easy railway ride
that lifts the tourists from Llanberis
while they're descending to Nant Peris.

The question we would like to ask
is what set business men to task
in making such a hideous mess
of this attractive wilderness.

The lure of monetary gain
will even cause a railway train
to climb the highest peak in Wales
to profit them when all else fails.

This quirk of man to spoil the earth
does not give Mother Nature mirth.
For worshiping the money god
she will not spare the awful rod.

It does seem very strange to me
that we should rape the land and sea
to over populate our kind.
God must now have a troubled mind.

J Perry

A Week Ago

Only a week ago,
As a budding flower,
Pain circled and stopped.
Now reborn through misty sight and ticking clock,
And straight line.
Magnetic eyes silenced,
Promises deaf,
In the moulded, plastic shell.

Only a week ago,
Tears and blood had a purpose,
Light was strong,
Line crooked,
Zig-zagging with the pulse,
While mouth sucked and sang
Without conscious love
From the tiny heart.

Only a week ago
I had so much to share.
Touching your cheek with the breeze,
Giggling with the trees.
Leaves have no mercy now,
But my love fills all space,
And it comforts me.

Only a week ago.

A week ago.

Claire Chilcott

On the Death of an Aunt

Quiet now, after life's struggle,
Struggle for life.
Peaceful now,
Heaven awaits a faithful servant.

No complaints at the burden to bear,
The cross to carry.
God's will has been done
Through a faithful servant.

Bustling and hurrying through life,
Each daily task a joy,
A helping hand, a kindness shown,
A heart fulfilled.

What a privilege to know that kindly soul.
To share the joys and sorrows
Of life's brimming cup
Ere tears o'erflow.

Quiet now, at peace, at rest
In heavenly love,
No pain or ills,
A true reward
For a faithful servant.

Margaret Hewitt

Double Back

For a reason
Inside unknown,
I he traced my path
Turning in the running,
From that gear
I couldn't cope,
My only way out
Was to get away,
Not able to walk past
So now I avoid it totally
Finding a new way home
The way of safety,
Not understanding the reaction
Out of control for a second,
The butterflies flew
Inside of me,
My heart galloped
For air,
My legs like a hurricane
Rushed until, out of sight.

Jodie L Daniels

Untitled

I sit here a feeble witness
to the slaughter of our Mother
poisoned and hacked to pieces
by her degenerate progeny.

The closer to the bone
the more the urge to desecrate
is amplified by the self disgust
of her lost generations

I sit here and do nothing
but wail helplessly
at my unwanted membership
of an insane species

Lobotomised by excess
emboldened by todays quick gain
blinded to tomorrows horrors
satisfied by nothing on earth.

Wandering through mists of opaque time
clutching at intuitions straws
fewer now them ever before
sniffing out Armageddon.

Grease my hair with oil-slick
wash my hands in acid
dizzy my eyes with electronic lies
and please God keep me placid

As above so below
I'm looking for the key
that starts the bus from the astral plane
to the terminus of me

Oh Isis, oh Osiris where are you now
now that I'm considering throwing in the Tao.

Plastic bags shall be our shroud
discarded tins our epitaph
not for us artifacts of Gold
or sweet mysteries of the shining path.

The planets shine with yesterdays glow
when they saturated all with vibrant power
I feel now they have crept away
disgusted by our basest hour

So follow me children
into the concrete abyss
and with trembling lip
await the Archous kiss.

John Sage

Judgement Day

What did you get out of life?
You the soldier, the grenadier
A medal or two,
Victory songs and tears.

What about you,
The scientist and brain?
A pat on the back and a
Peace prize.
For the nuclear bomb.

The songster, the liar,
The wife and child.
Add these to the
'Ordinary' list.

But wait, what's that?
Still living? Yes, a
Memory. Taking nothing from life,
But always giving.

Leave that to inherit the earth.

Leena Edmunds

The Birth of a Poem

Breathe deep, relax, don't push
- emerges naturally like a word jumble-sale
There's life and potential but what a mess!
clean it, dress it - make it look right
now display for all.

Nickie Manolescue

105

The Curtain Falls

First the darkness, then the light,
A place where I belong;
The dream I hold, of happiness here,
Will all too soon be gone.
In truth, I know, I see fantasies,
Viewed through eyes, half-closed and weak;
Yet as I lie here, alone and cold,
These deathly shadows I seek.
Mists swirl around, but there is nothing to fear,
I can rest now, and live on without pain;
Looking down, there is loneliness, many tears still to shed,
Feelings distant now, myself, never to be tormented again.
Death, my escape, His hand reaching out,
Willingly grasped by the hunted as I;
Yet mourned for we are, if not by many, by one,
Whose tears fall without end, for those gone, who still die.
The Earth is growing tired now,
The sun's fiery glow becomes dim;
Yet the Mother of Life must struggle on,
To fulfil the task set by Him.
Life, its purpose a mystery,
Many question it, and ask why carry on;
But a melody exists, although no answer it gives,
It's song life - The Show - Must Go on.
Believe...

Wendy

Talon Kissed

Slate blue lighting flashing from the skies
Taking away a mallards life
No more the fields and rivers to fly
Cut down as if by a godly knife
Stoops down so quiet, and mean
The slate and gold of the peregrine
A whisper of pity did she feel
For the life she had plucked away
Was it to be just one more meal
Forgotten as she flew away
But she can be forgotten, for the shadow that she cast
And every bird who feels her presence
Thinks that this day shall be it's last
The whole of Gods sky is her home
The clouds her floating walls
I hope forever her kind will roam
Through her blue and silver whispy halls
And to watch her in her glory
Wildly throwing her body through the mist
While her victims cut down and gory
Lie brokenly talon kissed
And flocks fly in fear
Everytime her shadow cast
Knowing that one of the flock
This day will be its last
Watch her as she silently falls
Through her blue and silver whispy halls
Again, again her shadow cast
For her quarry this day its last

C P Jennings

My Valley

The beauty of the vale where I live
The colourful array in nature's own pattern
The dew covered web's shining like satin
The sweet green grass luscious and bright
Waterfall's sparkling day and night
The pinewood forest's filling the air
Small fox cub's asleep deep in their lair
Bright blue sky not a cloud in sight
Rabbit's in the field swallows in flight
Look closely and you might see
The beauty of the valley the beauty to me.

Alan Prickett

Untitled

Poetry is a wondrous thing
To express ones thought with words that sing
Tis a gift for those who have the art
To speak and write, words from the heart

David Adrian Jenkins

Welsh Landscape

This is a landscape made by hands:
the cottages and disused quarry.
Ash, hawthorn, Rowan and the Wild service Tree.
a gate, a fence and daffodils are mine.

And in the County Archives one dusty afternoon
I tracked forgotten Williamses
who wheedled rocks from what would be fields
and built the honest, drystone walls.

The brown hill closes up the view
as I sit placing word on word.
From here we have all looked up
to the summit cairn for two thousand years.

Nameless are the small dark men
but I almost see them in the sea-scented mist
and, at the edge of hearing,
their voices whispers in the dusk.

They walked in procession up hill.
The funeral pyre stained the sky.
Then, with their hands, they built the cairn,
stone upon stone.

Shirley Jane Thomas

The Power

Power, ever moving, silent, unseen by the eye, like some unborn
                                                    Daughter
created from the dark, imposing, eternal, still reflective water
taken into the womb of machines that we have hidden beneath the
                                                    earth
Then finally discharged, sudden and electrifying is this birth

Perpetual or so it seems, transferred across the miles
To light the light, create the heat, that creates and lights the smiles
In the face of man who had now turned and protects this cherished
land
That over the ages he has all but destroyed by the harshness of his
hand

A new age will come when man has gone and all that will remain
Is his mark upon the earth, a dark acidic stain
But until this world has ended, until that final hour
If you listen you will still hear, the movement of the power.

Neil Bellamy

Forever Filled

Heavy snow close roadway.
No coalman, cold dismay
in the shed
Little amount coal lay
Burn bucket full each day.
on return.
Same amount of coal lay
Last until summer day.

Phyllis Blue

The Houses of the Valley

Reaching out in unending lines
Houses of the valleys, all the same
In their uniform of dereliction and decay
Clinging on to the hillside, like old people
Clinging on to the old way of life.

Smoke rises from the chimneys
Catching the last fading sunlight
of the promised summer of plenty,
Falling soon to the sills in black sooty smuts
Where sometimes people sit and stare.

The empty streets echo in the silence
of tack boots on the cobblestones,
Black windows stare at me with accusation
Betrayal screams at you with her evidence
in the houses of the valleys.

Ann Hughes

Cameo

Her watchful, roving eye
draw's my attention,
as I wait for the 'green'
on the Briwet bridge.

It belongs to a bird
on a makeshift nest,
blending with the ballast of the railway track.

This Midsummer Day,
I move my car,
and pretend to look
at the shampooed shore with its tints of pink.

The bridge vibrates
A drama unfolds.
Bird's head dives inside her plumage.
All I see when the train has gone,
is a bird serene,
with an orange bill, and twinkling eye.

John Linares

114

A Tinsel Princess

She's only a tinsel Princess
Who sits on a golden throne,
For this she squandered her freedom,
Now leads no life of her own.

She rules in remote isolation
From her vantage point on high,
She's duty bound to her station
As the train of life passes by.

She's only a tinsel Princess
Who leads the glittering show,
What pomp and ceremony can't impress
Cruel power will overthrow.

A prison is still a prison
Though it look like a golden throne;
When the sparkle clouds your vision
Then your freedom's no longer your own.

A J Macdonald

Reflections

The door slams shut
And I am left alone.
How long since you preferred
The Boot to compromise?
The white lace and red rose
As crushed as yesterday's kiss.

Jones

Abermenai

Over there;
across the flats
where sandpipers wade
and quarrelsome curlews call,
stubborn marram dunes
buffer the westerlies
that once swelled mizens and royals
running for Abermenai road.

Over there;
glistening yachts strain at their anchors
while weekend sailors
loudly announce their escape
from the concrete kingdoms
beyond The Dyke;
their piercing haughty cries
defiant in the wind.

Over there;
amidst the fostered farms
and adopted cottages
the Cymry blissfully ape
an alien twang;
ignoring Dwynwen's moans
and the mute Llanfaglan bell
which has lost its 'tongue'.

Ken Lloyd Gruffydd

Another Diet

The more I think about losing weight,
The more I pile upon my plate.
The more I look in the mirror and see,
The more depressed I get about me.
I've tried all the diet's that you can name,
It's just that I hate the starvation pain.
I wish I had the will-power to fight,
Instead of eating night after night.
I'd like to lose quite a few stone,
Start to exercise and begin to tone.
I'd like to have the perfect figure,
Instead of feeling bigger and bigger.
they tell us to eat smaller quantities.
instead of a hoard.
But I know I eat because I'm bored.
I'm going to try and try again
It's just that I hate the starvation pain.

Helen Hough

A Night in the Victoria Wood

Shadows flitting in the night
And flames consuming pinewood,
The owl speaks and branches creak
Reflected moon in silver stream
Flows silent through the dark
To find it's way to Peris deep
And down to Padarn-sleeping
The ghosts of by gone days come creeping
To nestle by my crackling fire
And share a can of nectar sweet,
'Neath starlit roof I slumber deep
Water laced with morning sun
And bee filled noises flying
Warm grey embers lying, dying
A life a soul awakening.

J Foulkes

The Black Hen

She will not go into the henhouse tonight,
I find her, blinking in the torchlight,
Huddled in a favourite dustbath,
Between the old tractor and the barn.
Her feathers turn the amber beam to greens and blues,
Yet even in it's unnatural warmth, her comb shrivels palely.
She moves,
I hear the feathers press against her screaming bones,
I know what I should do,
She knows I cannot do it,
Cannot, will not, it hardly matters.
And so tonight, she waits in dust and moonlight,
Draped in her greens and blues, for iridescent death.
And be it fox or frost, it hardly matters,
It will be welcome.
She shuffles in a darkness that can never yield to day.
I take one last look,
Hold one last image,
An image I will use in daylight to set aside my sorrow,
In darkness to set aside my weakness.
Then turning the torch upon the treacherous ground,
I move towards the unsympathetic house,
hoping that what goes round...
... comes round.

Rosemarie Sheehan

The Birthday Card

The shaking hand that traced the wiry letters
traced the future:
that caressed my hair when I was young
now grips my heart with grief.
And I am left to wonder -
Did you know too?

Hands more eloquent than words their joints gnarled
like old branches
their sinews stretched with time
tell the story of a life long-lived.
And I am left to wonder -
Do you know too?

The emptiness of future anniversaries
flashed before me;
Words of love, not for this day alone
but for all the days to come.
And I no longer wonder -
You do know too.

Frances Cummins

121

Reason

They say there is a reason
They say that time will heal
But neither time or reason
Will change the way I feel
For no-one know's the heartache
That lies behind my smile
no-one know's how many times
I have broken down and cried
I want to tell you something
So there won't be any doubt
Your so wonderful to be with
and yet so hard to be without
So they say this is a Reason
and that time will heal
But I know I will never change
never change the way I feel
There is no other to take your place
The length of time were apart
For your love is still in my heart.
So is this, they say a reason
and that time will heal
But I know that time or reason
Will never change the way I feel.

S Burton

Heart Attack

All day, a vague persistent feeling
That something was amiss.
Routine tasks usually accomplished
without effort or exertion,
Had left me ill at ease and wearied.
Then, my friend arrived
All cheerfulness and chatter,
Day-time cares forgotten in the bustle
of serving a companionable meal.
An evening spent in cosy gossip
Dressing gowned and slippered by the fire.
Then, bedtime and once again
That pause of foreboding and disquiet
Was it real or imagined.
That sudden onset of pain and laboured breathing?
No! No! Gasping and choking, I struggle to my friend,
Sleeping and unaware of my distress
A frantic phone call brings reassurance.
Doctor's on his way
I struggle to keep up the fight for breath
The, the awful realisation,
'So this is what it's like to die'.
My Doctor comes calm and competent,
The needles plunge bring swift relief.
I breathe again, and quietly drift
Into the blessed sleep of forgetfulness
And, as pale beams of morning sun
Come sliding through my window,
I slowly wake and breathe a prayer of thankfulness
Dear God! I'm still alive.

Dorothy M Collier

How Awful

How awful are the green
slimy waters
of the Mill field weir.
Appearing in effervescent bublets
of thickening sludge,
like snot, with a consistency of ice-cream.

Yet fish
live there, or so I'm told.
By Christ,
am I never amazed?
My eyes glaze at the thought.

Patricia Lewis

Trains

To you or me
just one fat tea trolley lady
or another.
One a little plumper than the other
maybe,
voluminous tits
bulging out of all sides of her
bra.
Short blonde hair,
plump face,
short sleeved white blouse,
navy skirt.

But to the plump, chortling train guard with the merry brown
eyes
and dark brown hair,
one he played with,
one he didn't.

One plump woman excited him
into
cavorting up and down the corridor between the seats,
throwing and catching bags of sugar,
and playing in the guards compartment.

The other one
he didn't even see.
I only have eyes for you,
plump pink giggling teasing tea lady.

She couldn't know it
but her guard was faithful.
His dimples and plump arms came alive for her.
He was not unfaithful with the tea lady
who got on with her trolley
to carry on the journey
to Crewe.

Penny Stempel

Aberfan Child

Wrathful rolling clouds
Slag grey, ash grey
A storm is boiling o'er our hills tonight
Late lights only at the chapel windows
Prelude to a day of doom
The clanging utgorn sounding
Solemn brazen trumpet, polished ready
About to blow God's glorious ire
And fling it at our hills.

I was but a child,
Afraid of the giants, of
Elephantine apparitions rumbling
Mustering to march on our horizon

wishing it were just a childish dream
A half-remembered picnic
Not wanting it to signal
Gigantic intervention in my life.

Wanting to grow up and
Sport on our hills, to
Wave a rude red rag,
A bloody banner
Be a hero, win a freedom
Chasing birds across the hills.
But not to be a cornered mole
In terror of the barn owl
Of flapping wings about to pounce...

...Where is our hill?
The trump I'd heard was the last
For us at least;

Our hill is down, our world unmade
And all our bones in prison under it:
Terror of a trapped and taken soul.

Hywel Jeremiah

Life

I really do no think
that we, people of today
appreciate our lives enough
appreciate our very short stay
on this earth of ours
as it really is so short,
it passes by so quickly
I really think we ought
not to wish it away
as we so often do
I think we're all guilty of this
Yes, me and you.
During our working day
how often do we say
I'll be glad when home time comes?
and look forward to the end of the day?
On Mondays we often think
'I wish the weekend was here!
and it arrives before we know it,
then again, Monday is very near.
When the winter months begin
with snow and hail and rain
We wish the time away
to see summer again.
We should make the most of life,
just take it day by day
as it only comes around once
and it is not a very long stay.

Karen James-Rees

Davies

Davies? I knew him for more then twenty years,
well, I didn't really know him, not that close,
never actually found out what it was that
made him 'tick' as they say.

I never succeeded in probing beyond
that strange silent exterior of his.
Davies was a loner, lived alone, no family.
Work, it seemed, his only interest.

Not once did I see him read a book or newspaper.
He never discussed politics, religion, sex, not anything
what caused him to be passed over by life's cruel contempt?
Often I speculated, had he some dark secret?
Scarred memories of a bitter past? jilted
at the altar perhaps in his youth?

Once over a drink, I caught a fleeting glimpse
of the inner Davies. Defences briefly breached by beer
and melancholy, he confided that he was afraid of close
relationships. Always pain at the end of it,
he argued; even a pet cat or dog brought hurt.

Davies retired last year, left characteristically
without ceremony. Walked out after some thirty years.
No handshakes, no goodbyes not even a solemn
shrug of the shoulders, nothing.

I met him once or twice for a drink, then missed him.
Heard he'd been ill, taken to hospital, 'put away'
the less kind said. His house, they say was full of
plastic bags, hundred of them, scattered about like
societies dejected offerings, discarded, unwanted,
a sort of caricature of himself.

130

I visited him once only in hospital, that was the
last time I saw him. There he was, standing in front
of the window with a fearful look on his face,
eyes thyrotoxic searching the skies and muttering
something about the coming of Christ.

Poor old bugger, his mind had gone you see!

Lionel Griffiths

Penmon At Midnight

The stars surfed through a watery sky,
The lighthouse winked like a peep show sign,
The pebbles cackled beneath my feet,
As I walked towards the whispering sea.

tranquillity caressed my trembling body,
As the waves placed a kiss upon the shore;
When the virgin moon lit the awe in my eyes
She saw the thief that stole me.

Sheena-Jane Macfarlane

132

Untitled

Love is a feeling within a soul
but is felt within a heart
Love is a power stronger than time
that can tear two lives apart
Love is the truth known only to man,
a gift we must learn to share
A voice that is spoken without any words,
expressed to show we care
Love is a thought, a pain, a cry,
an innocent feeling of guilt
And when love dies, like ice bitten flowers
our hearts will freeze and wilt

Heather Paterson

Anger

The atmosphere was troubled,
the mood hostile.
Tension had been building all day, in the heavy air.
And then, one careful word, misjudged,
broke the banks.
The dam burst. Not a trickle to stream to a river,
but a rushing torrent, bursting forth.
Hot angry words, insults jibes.
Old grievances and past troubles aired.
New annoyances formed.
Screaming and yelling,
shouting and swearing.
Caught in a blind, red rage, in a meaningless fury,
no thoughts, just instinct.
Things said that were never meant,
biting to the core,
and other words, straight from the heart
glanced off, un-noticed.
the anger built, loud and hot,
swirling and rising, pulling and pushing
to insane peaks.
and then it was over;
as if a bell had rung.
They retreated - to lick their wounds.
The anger was gone,
leaving an emptiness that was not peace.
Silence reigned supreme.

Mhairi Jensen (14)

Searching for the Answer

Who was I?
Where did I go?
Did I survive in the fast lane
Or exist in the slow?

Was I good, bad or indifferent
To life and my fellow man?
Living independently rich,
Or was I pale and wan?

Were my children paternally
The fruit of my loins
Or maternally conceived?
What was the plan of the last role
So intricately weaved?

Who were the souls
That surrounded the
Individual of me?
Were my abilities overpowering
Or did I continue forth
Unable to see?

I want to know the answer
To the question of the form.
I know who I am when I die,
But cannot remember
When I am born.

Jo Newton

Never Again

I get up in the morning
It's sickness that I feel
If we could just buy babies
That would be ideal

Everything gets larger
Tender feeling breasts
You find it hard to work
All you want to do is rest

Your stomach quickly hardens
A lump there soon appears
No matter how you try
You can't ignore your fears

The father to be is happy
Can't wait to spread the news
If they felt what we women felt
they'd permanently have the blues

As the months slowly pass
You find it hard to move
Not very long to go now
Then things will improve

Then suddenly you feel a twitch
And water starts to pour
The pain is just incredible
You can't take anymore

When you're about to give up
You hear a sudden scream
Then you have a beautiful baby
And it all seems like a dream

Michelle Roberts

Bakelite Wireless

Your Art Deco geometry squats
like a thunderbox, but less musical.
My imagination mass-produces
Mozart in lumps, each movement
evacuated painfully. Utilitarian
too, Mozart manufactured
six concertos in a year. Plastic
should be so durable.

Off-switch a symmetrically-placed
blob, a turn-off consistent
with your design, it makes only
your sound go away. So apt
for forecasts of foul weather,
declarations of war, you served
an audience by making bombs
seem sonorous.

For you, conservationists
destroy, antique shops
lower prices. You lump of unloveliness.
You epitome of earache. Gaucheness
solidified. Almost attractive enough
to call ugly, you're a monument
to malformation, interference
a relief, a long-wave warning
of cathode rays to come, a pseudo-
scientific artefact whose society
is concrete and novelty: the industrialist
as artist.

Neal Mason

The Old Deal

Darkness corrupts the memories of a day,
For the child, huddled in a pillow
Against the militant coalition
Of streetlight shade and coloured walls.

In the corner, behind the wardrobe,
It's just a shadow, just like yesterday.
But the sounds are real enough,
He just can't throw them off.

A toss to the crash of jet engine,
A turn to the crackle of a probable hit
Somewhere in the distance , a back bedroom
Just like his, and the screams.

Too much late horror, she said, the silly
Screams, but he can't throw them off.
Sand blows through the pulled up sheets and
Leaves conspire in the garden.

While curtains remonstrate in an open roof,
Mother gurgles downstairs over a glass
Of warm, red wine, giggling,
Perhaps as a television tragi-comedy.

It's alright again when day breaks
Into long clear lines along the sandy
Garden path. Through the sheets
The steadfast, mellow, wardrobe

Blows to pieces all over my little brother,
But it's no problem. I'll pull back the tall
Silk curtains and smile on the blue of the day
And the cool, green fields of England.

Mervyn Ray

Mythical Love

Come, o'h come again
My mythical love,
Come once again
In my dream.
Let your gentle hands
Caress me
Whisper sweet nothings
In my ear.
How I long
To feel your nearness
As I in time
Let past years fade
And I am once again
In youthful bliss
With that enchanting moment
Reliving the memory
Of our very first kiss.
Nectar was never sweeter
Like wine soaring in my veins
Setting my heart on fire
The flame thro' life it retains.
Flickering like a candle
Afraid of the fading gleam
I call once again to my love
Come back, come back
Once again
If not in life, I surrender
Myself to a mythical dream.

Olive Samuel

Old Man in a Wheelchair

Old, ages old.
Contours contort the eyes
Into a soulful stare
Of ancient memories and dreams.

A cigarette held between lips
That spoke a million words
And laughed a thousand laughs
And cried too many cries.

In a war that took life from life
He battled and won
And lost a love to another
But held no bitterness or shame.

On a day clear and calm
An accident broke his body
It shattered and cracked
Leaving him paralysed in pain.

Now this day or tomorrow
He sits to contemplate life
It's mysteries and illusions
And waits for the end.

Neil Cunningham

Waiting

I sat on the bench
All alone on that very cold day,
Clutching a beautiful array
of flowers
For her, when from the train,
She makes her way.

Slowly the train came rumbling in
And I stood up excitedly
Her eyes met mine unknowingly.
I then ran to her shouting with glee
Mummy, Mummy,
Mummy it's me.

Margaret O Jones

Women's Lies

This old dress?
Why I've had it for years
And you haven't noticed
Remembering how I smuggled it in
Only yesterday
And hid the bag behind the settee
While you made tea

How much did it cost?
It was in a sale
I didn't think you would mind
Remembering how I wrote the cheque
And duly signed
And ripped off the label
When I told you the fable

Was that lovemaking good?
Of course my darling
I am really fulfilled
Remembering how I'd panted and writhed
Only minutes before
When it was so boring
Before you were snoring

And my fortnight in Spain
Just me and the girls
What a miserable time
Remembering his dark flashing eyes
As he fondled my thighs
At the airport I kissed you
And vowed that I missed you
And just hated Spain
And would not go again
Do I like your best mate?
The one that you drink with
I can't stand him dear, always smelling of beer
Remembering Spain, and that soft Spanish bed
Where he drank wine instead.

Jan Price

The Pub

Chatty, smoky, okey dokey
'What's yours love?'
'The usual please.'
Ringing till and curling smoke
Roaring laughter; what's the joke?
Hazy people, happy people
Lonely people gathered here
Does collective warmth and closeness
Help allay unspoken fear?
Clinking ice and fizzing lemon
Crackling crisps and we're in heaven
Aren't we?

Rosemary Johns

Final Performance

I've been in hospital for the second time.
They must like me as their guest.
They even had me in on Sunday.
Dressed in my 'Sunday Best'.
On Monday it was down the theatre.
For the second show.
First time it was rehearsal.
I'm glad I didn't know.
But now I think I'm on the mend.
With all the stitches out.
But no repeat performance, no encores.
This Dame is bowing out.

M Hilliard

One of the Pleasures of Shopping

As she walks with grace from place to place
Moving so smoothly pace after pace,
She looks quite at ease,
And happy to please,
Inner glow giving warmth to her face.

This is amply revealed in her eyes
-The term tender so aptly applies-
A look that provokes,
The hope it evokes,
And gives rise to delicious surmise.

Simply standing still she's a delight,
An arresting and heart - warming sight.
It's a joy to observe
The swell and the curve
Which are each so erotically right.

The happiness felt is a measure
Of how work re-forms into pleasure.
It can only be
To see such as she
That makes shopping feel one's at leisure.

Denys Andrews

Ground Frost

The last leaves
Defiant in their rigor mortis.

Slow trickle of the sinus,
Flinty intake

And yew hedges iced with it.

The stare of the farmer's wife
As the young girl behind the till
Hands back the wrong change.

Suzanne Iuppa

Broken Time

Seems sad somehow,
Never again that golden chain
Stretched across that precious paunch.
No more Grandfatherly hands
Reaching for tiny Grandson's ones.
Even the watch has no hands now.
Cannot even express; feel.
Solid gold still surrounds
It's innards' intrinsic beauty:
Beauty begging recognition.
Still willing to serve.
No-one to see, take, work, watch.
Seems sad somehow.

Sue Nelson

Sadness

It came like a thief but what it stole
was much more precious than money or gold.
For what it stole was my friends mind
oh why did life treat her so unkind.
Now with her mind gone
she finds it so hard to carry on
and talks only of days gone by
and people who have long since died.
I know no matter what ever I do
she will never be like she use to.
And it's so sad to stand by
watching while she just cries
and what ever comfort I may give
sometimes she says she doesn't want to live
but no matter, come what may
I will love and care for her night and day.

Eileen Kyte

Free Spirit

To soar like a seagull,
Lonely, on high,
Gliding, in gold,
In the evening sky,
With only the breeze,
And the rays of the sun,
And the sound of the sea,
'Til his day is done;
Wheeling and diving
With effortless grace:
Would I were a bird
To be in his place.

Dorothy Neil

St Mary Street - Cardiff

Seagulls fuss low in the opaque sky -
Swooping, diving, feathering
Over the heads of those who pass by
In busy St Mary street:
I stand at a bus stop
My laden basket at my feet
Watching their white-winged antics
Over the roofs and chimney tops
Of cheek by jowl Cardiff shops:
Then I hear the mournful wail
Of fog-sirens
Complaining to ships
Of mists
From nearby old Tiger Bay
That stirs in me an age-old hiraeth
As I know the waters of the Channel
Arc in -
To protect my Cymric home
And fix a Celtic boundary
Over which -
As the threshold mewing sea-gulls -
I do not want to go...

Kathleen Daugela

Jolly Roger

The taverns stone steps
They're very well worn,
Sizzling sunshine
A quaint cobbled road.

The cave in a cliff face,
An old Pirates cove,
A winding worn path,
Leads from the seashore.

Imagining movements
From long ago,
Muffled and swaggering
To the contraband stores.

Shimmering silks
Whisky galore,
Brandy and Gin casks
With rum left on board.

Then sailing away,
To plunder once more,
Ships on the high sea,
Or a foreign shore.

Filled full with booty,
They sail home once more
Hugging the coastline
They'd make for the cove.

Norrie Hill

Lovers Parting

Just give me one more kiss before we part
That we may bosom friends forever be,
Then put all thoughts of passion firmly by
Love must never bloom for you and me.

My world is full and happy, I'm content
With all that life has freely given me;
You too have reaped true happiness
'Till now - so we must let things be.

We did not ask fate to intervene
But lovers we could so easily be;
So go your way though don't forget we met
And your heart will always hold a part of me.

Frances Chaffey

Pit Closure

They're closing the pit wail who have never
Been in the dark, coughed up black spit.

They're closing the pit moan those who have never
Entered the cage felt their gut hit their brain.

They're closing the pit moan those who have never
Crawled on their bellies, tasted coal in their mouth.

They're closing the pit worry those who have never
Sweated in seams, rubbed the dust from their eyes.

They're closing the pit cry those who have never
Been buried alive, heard gases explode.

They're closing the pit say those that have never
Been drowned in a passage, lost and arm or a leg.

They're closing the pit say the men with the blue scars
Gasp the men who are dying, groan the men who are maimed.

They're closing the pit sing the souls of the miners
Buried down deep, you can hear them all laugh.

They're closing the pit, the wheel isn't turning
The cage just hangs empty, this graveyard is closed.

Margaret Lloyd

Gone

He died. You do not look for wisdom
or religion or spiritual remainders,
you know no more.
We join you as you scream at images
of twisted beauty broken on a pavement,
of presence, of uniqueness, thrown away.

Unbidden, we consider, no comfort,
the triviality of death continued,
of precious fragments of humanity
reflecting an ever ever fragility
through turning yearning years
where past mothers look with low-lid eyes
on memories of children decimated,
each as love-inspiring as the last.

We try to smile at thoughts of all he did,
all he brought into our lives
We find no comfort, yet still we smile
to honour him.
Our grief could destroy him:
we keep him alive.

Richard Holland

The Sparrow

A pair of buzzards wheel and soar
Above the trees, across the moor.
Two sparrows in a garden small,
Flit, to a bush, beneath the wall.
One hurts its wing-a garden cord
Hung from a branch across the sward-
Hops on the lawn, calls to its mate
sounds an alarm-but tis' too late!
The eyes that see the sparrow fall,
The buzzard; swoop beneath the wall.
That which sustains all life on earth
Does not exclude the buzzards worth.

Trevor Lewis

Life is it a Waste?

Man's life is like a cloud that fades and is gone,
Man dies and never returns,
Forgotten by all who knew him,
So he continually strives to make his mark whilst he is on this Earth,
So that he will be remembered in centuries to come,
Defaming people as he strives for success,
Foolishly gathering riches that he cannot take with him,
We were born as nothing,
And we will die as nothing.

Wendy Tina Jones

Those Strong Arms

I truly loved your arms,
They would always protect me.
If I was cold
They would warm me.
If I was scared
They would hold me.
When I was hurt
They defended me.

I can't believe those same arms
Shook me, battered me
And destroyed me.
Say they weren't your arms
But someone else's.

Mary Kaye

Childhood Games

I close my eyes and see the days
of childhood games and faces,
Fair haired girls with bouncing curls
And boys all running races.
We played house with china cups
To teach our dolls nice ways,
But oh! Those aggravating boys
Would interrupt our play,
Their whoops and cries did echo
round the cowboy, Indian slain;
When Saturday morning pictures
They would re-enact again.

Now my eyelids flutter open
The cries sound real enough,
I peep out through my window
Where the game to me looks tough.
Mud splattered legs and faces
Kick and scrabble for the ball,
Who's in charge there is no sign
But the writing's on the wall.
What happened to the bouncing curls
With rough and tumble boys?
They grew up in another world,
Here, equality needs no toys.

Shirley Silman

Observations. Transformations. Art and Death

Art hangs in the corner, observed only by its creator.
An orange towel drying, draped over easel, metamorphosising,
motionless yet flowing, a time warp glowing.
Becomes a distant mountain sculptured in cotton.
is a Van Gogh study, silently swirling...
a woven fibre sunflower surrounded by sunflowers,
growing together... together... together.

Tomorrow-o-tomorrow.
Anti-stress nutrients, strata and snow filled landscapes
that were once volcanoes,
erupt into my dreams, where sheep and cattle do vain battle
with Radio One and the abattoirs' own nightmare
production line horror show...
Skinned alive and still kicking, it's dead enough by dinner time.

Dinner time and more metamorphic earth-shattering news,
as volcanic lava, the boiling over - tired of being exploited -
blood of Gaia is thrust through my conservationist's calender.
The living colour picture pages erupt simultaneously
in stripped pine kitchens throughout the calender collecting world.
A surreal conspiracy, unleashed against the Greens, backfires
as a gigantic cloud of volcanic dust gathers in the stratosphere
blotting out the sun forever.
No sun equals no solar powered alternative industries.
But wait, no sun equals no industries, the end of all life forms,
no light, no art, endless dark... ahhh. I run outside to check the sky.

Counting a quick six.
I observe the midnight meteor entering Earth's atmosphere,
incinerate, at one thousand miles per second, burning, burning,
burning through space a path equivalent on Earth
from San Fransisco to New York, in three to four seconds.
The time it takes to die.

161

Starved of sleep, we sheep hear slaughtering knives blunted on bone:
we're standing in excrement, ankle deep, shivering.
No compassion between man and beast here,
only suffering, neglect, violence and fear.
We weep for our fellow companions as their blood showers our skins
We're trapped in terror to wait in turn for the stabbing electrode,
the nerve shattering stick and sickening still life,
framed in a window, hung on a butcher's hook.

Robin Richards